The Good Green Lunchbox

Words and recipes by Jocelyn Miller

Photography by John Williams

Illustration by Richard Deverell

Contents

LION

Cooking: the rules

• Always ask a grown-up for permission to cook. Ask them to help you use knives and the cooker safely.

• Start with a clean and tidy kitchen... and leave it clean and tidy.

• Wash your hands before handling foodstuffs, and rinse them frequently while working.

• Protect your clothes with an apron.

• Tie back long hair.

• Wear shoes that will protect your feet if you drop anything.

1 Picnic bag

This is a book about making fantastic food for lunches and picnics. These recipes are good because they're good for you and green because they're easy on the planet.

But first of all… what are you going to put your lunch in? If you have a lunchbox, simply reuse it. Or you can make this easy softbox to carry all shapes and sizes of things in reused containers.

You can use any strong woven fabric. The one shown here is jute sacking.

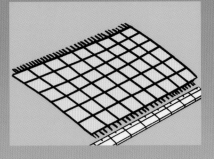

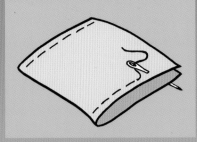

1 Measure a rectangle of fabric 30cm x 50cm. Be sure it is "square" with the weave.

2 Fold right sides together and join the sides with a strong in-and-out stitch.

3 Squash the corners as shown and stitch across. This gives the bag a box shape.

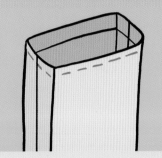

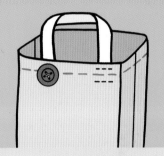

4 Turn the bag right side out and fold the top edge over. Stitch in place.

5 Cut lengths of stout tape for the handles. Stitch in place. Decorate the join as you wish: perhaps with bright buttons.

Avoid using disposable napkins by making your own out of fabric that can be washed and reused. You can recycle a good bit of an outgrown garment to make the napkin.

2 Good green sandwich

Every lunchbox needs a healthy and tasty sandwich –
this one is perfect. The quantities given make
two sandwiches.

4 slices of chunky brown
  bread
1 large avocado
1 tomato
½ lime
1 tablespoon olive oil
salt and pepper
salad leaves (optional)

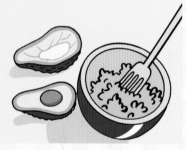

1 Spoon the avocado
flesh into a bowl and
mash with a fork.

2 Chop the tomato into
tiny pieces. Add to the
avocado.

3 Squeeze the lime.
Add the juice, salt, and
pepper. Mix.

4 Spread the mix onto
one slice of bread. Throw
on a few salad leaves and
sandwich it all together.

Raising animals for meat
or dairy products uses
a lot more energy and
produces more carbon
dioxide (the gas that
causes climate change)
than simply growing plants.
Plant-based foods are also
packed full of the vitamins
you need to be healthy.

Wrap it up! Use a sheet of cellophane to wrap your sandwiches as shown, and tie with a scrap of ribbon or string. Cellophane is a good green material because it's biodegradable – that means it will eventually decay like a potato peeling instead of hanging around for hundreds of years like a plastic bag.

3 Beanburger

This beanburger is good and green because, like the sandwich (page 2), it is veggie – kind to animals and kind to the planet. You could eat it as it is or pop it into a burger bun and add some salad leaves and chopped tomato. Makes two.

40g cooked kidney beans
40g cooked butter beans
3cm carrot, grated
1/8 grated onion
2 tablespoons olive oil
large squeeze of tomato puree
30g mixed nuts, finely chopped
1 teaspoon coriander (optional)

1 Mash the two sorts of beans in a bowl with a fork until you have a lumpy paste.

2 Fry the grated onion and carrot with 1 tablespoon of oil on a low heat for about 2 minutes.

3 Add the mashed beans, nuts, tomato puree, and spice. Mix together.

The hummus dip on page 7 makes a delicious relish.

4 Take the pan off the heat and leave to cool. Roll the mixture into two balls and flatten slightly to make burger shapes.

5 Fry the burgers in the other spoonful of oil for a few minutes until slightly crisp on each side.

Burger box: For that burger bar look, wrap your burger in greaseproof paper and pop it into a homemade box.

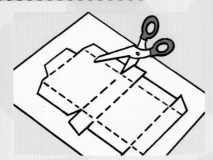

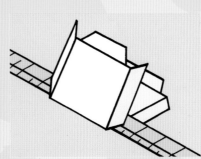

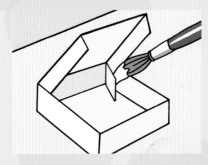

1 Copy the template on the back of this book onto a sheet of card and cut it out.

2 Fold along the dotted lines using a ruler.

3 Assemble as shown by gluing the tabs to the sides of the box.

4 Pizza pod

Pizza is delicious but it's not your usual lunchbox fare because it's so floppy. However, these pizza pods are easily transported and, stuffed with vegetables, they are good, green, and healthy too. Makes four pizza pods.

500g bread flour – ½ white and ½ wholemeal makes a nice mix
300ml warm water (dip your finger in – it should feel as if it's the same temperature as the air)
1 sachet of fast-action yeast
3 tablespoons olive oil
2 teaspoons salt
½ teaspoon sugar
your choice of filling – tomato puree, pepper, mushroom, cheese, sweetcorn…

Just wrap a pod in greaseproof paper and a napkin (see page 1) and it's ready to go.

1 To make the dough:
Mix together the flour,
salt, sugar, yeast, and oil
in a large bowl.

2 Pour in the warm water
gradually, mixing the
dough as you go. Then
tip the dough onto a
clean work surface.

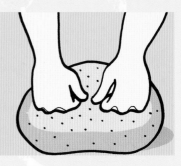

3 Knead the dough
until springy enough to
bounce back when you
poke it. This should take
around 10 minutes.

You can freeze the
spare dough – just
remember to take it
out to defrost before
you bake it.

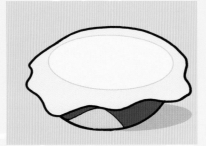

4 Wash and dry the bowl
and swirl a little olive
oil inside. Then add the
dough, cover with a tea
towel, and leave to rise
in a warm place until it is
double the size: about 1
hour.

5 Divide the dough into
four equal–sized balls.
Roll one ball into a circle
the size of a plate. Cover
one half with your choice
of filling.

6 Fold it over and then
press the edges tightly
together. If you're feeling
creative, decorate the top
with sprigs of rosemary.
Bake in the oven at 180°C
for 12 minutes or until a
light gold colour.

5 Seasonal soup

A bowl of hot soup is the perfect lunch for a cold, windy day. Here are two types of soup – leeky and squashed – for different seasons of the year. Squashes are in season in the autumn and leeks are at their best at the end of winter.

Makes four small servings.

With the leftover dough from your pizza pods (on page 4), bake small bread rolls to have with your hot winter soup.

Carry in an insulated flask.

1 Chop the garlic, onion, and other vegetables.

2 Fry the onion and garlic with the oil on a low heat in a large pan.

3 Add the other vegetables into the pan and then cover with boiling water. Stir in the stock cube.

4 Cover with a lid and leave to simmer for about 15 minutes or until the vegetables are soft.

5 Drain the vegetables, keeping the stock in a jug.

6 Blend the vegetables in the pan using a hand blender, pour in half of the stock, and whizz until smooth. Add the cream and give it another quick whizz.

1 small onion
1 clove of garlic
1 tablespoon olive oil
1 vegetable stock cube
either 1 leek and 1 medium potato
 OR ½ large butternut squash
100ml single cream

See page 16 for more information on seasonal produce.

6 Grow your own salad

Growing your own food is the super-green number-one best way of getting good green food. It uses less energy because it doesn't have to travel miles and miles to your plate, and it's fun too!

salad seeds – including
    lettuce, rocket, and mustard
shallow tray – an old fruit
    punnet is suitable
soil (or use some homemade
    compost)

1 Line the bottom of the tray with 2cm of soil. Sprinkle your seeds evenly over the soil.

2 Cover the seeds with another 1cm layer of soil, then water.

3 Water your salad regularly so that the soil doesn't dry out but be careful not to let it get waterlogged. After about two weeks, your leaves should be ready to pick.

Mix your salad leaves together with other fresh salad ingredients such as tomatoes and peppers and transport them in a little box. Remember to pack a fork.

You don't need a garden. These micro salad leaves can also grow happily on a sunny window sill.

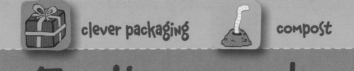

8 Fruit capsules

Some fruits, such as bananas, come pre-wrapped in their skins and travel easily. But grapes and slices of melon and pineapple aren't so easy to transport – that is, if you don't have a fruit capsule. Make one out of old plastic drinks bottles.

Try to find two bottles of the same size that curve inwards at the middle. Get a grown-up to help you and trim off any jagged edges.

2 empty soft drink bottles
your choice of fresh fruit

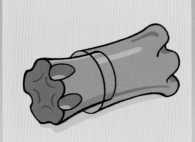

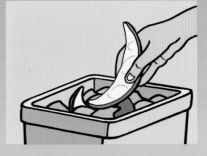

1 To make your capsule: Cut the top off two bottles so you have one tall and one short end.

2 Squish the edges of the short bottle slightly with your fingers so it fits into the larger one.

3 Wash your fruit. Peel and cut your fruit up as necessary. Compost the leftovers.

Your capsule can be used to carry other things – nuts, raisins, or anything else you like.

Put your unwanted seeds, tough skins, and stalks left over from your fruit in a compost bin. They will break down over several months to make crumbly "soil". This can be used to help grow vegetables. Note: don't put cooked food or animal products (including egg shells) into your compost bin.

9 Real fruit yoghurt

This is a super-tasty and super-green recipe which you can make from local, freshly picked fruit. Use raspberries or blackberries when they're in season, in the summertime. Pick-your-own farms and farmers' markets are good places to get fresh berries. This recipe makes one generous serving.

50g fresh raspberries or blackberries – that's about 10 berries
100g plain yoghurt
¼ teaspoon vanilla essence

Don't pick wild berries unless a grown-up is there to guide you. Not all berries are safe to eat.

1 Squish the berries into a pulp with the back of a spoon.

2 In a small bowl, mix the berries into the yoghurt.

3 Add the vanilla essence and stir. Spoon the yoghurt into a pot to take in your lunchbox.

As a winter alternative to summer berries, try fresh mango. Mash a few slices of fairtrade mango and add a splash of lime instead of vanilla essence.

Reuse empty peanut butter, jam, and honey jars to carry your yoghurt in. Remember to wash them out thoroughly first, and after every use. Keep your yoghurt cool until lunchtime. Carry an icepack in your lunchbox.

10 Homemade lemonade

Little bottles and cartons may be convenient for lunchboxes but they are certainly not good for our planet. Avoid the packaging of single servings by making your own tasty drinks and refilling your own bottle. This will really help to reduce the amount of rubbish you throw away. Makes two small servings.

500ml water
1 lemon
½ lime
5 tablespoons sugar

Crush a few raspberries into the mix for pink lemonade.

1 Squeeze the lemon and lime juice into a jug. Add the sugar.

2 Boil the water, pour into the jug, and stir. Put in the fridge to cool down – add ice if you are impatient!

The rubbish that we can't compost or recycle will usually end up in landfill – great pits of rubbish that may take hundreds of years to break down.

Take your lemonade to school in a bottle. Wash out an old bottle and refill it each day. You could even make your own label.

This recipe shows you how much sugar there is in a sweet drink. Be sure to make it only as a treat and choose plain tap water for every day.

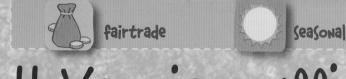
11 Veggie muffins

It might seem a bit wacky to put vegetables in muffins, but these really are delicious. The courgettes for this recipe will be in season from late summer. You could try growing your own!

1 Grate the courgettes.

2 Put the eggs, sugar, oil, and vanilla essence into a bowl and mix thoroughly.

3 Add the flour, baking soda, salt, and cinnamon to the bowl and mix.

4 Add the grated courgette and nuts and stir.

5 Put a large spoonful of mixture into muffin cases so that each one is just over half full.

6 Put the muffins in the oven at 160°C for about 15 minutes or until golden brown on top.

2 small courgettes (or 1 large)
2 free-range eggs
175g brown sugar
150ml sunflower oil
2 teaspoons vanilla essence
250g self-raising flour
1 teaspoon baking soda
1 teaspoon salt
1 teaspoon cinnamon
50g chopped walnuts or pecans
   (optional)

Silicone muffin cases are great because they are reusable.

These muffins are easy to transport. Just wrap in greaseproof paper and a napkin (see page 1).

12 Fairtrade fridgecake

Use fairtrade chocolate to make this delicious treat and look out for fairtrade nuts, dried fruit, and biscuits too. Can you make this an entirely fairtrade treat?

100g dark chocolate
65g butter
1 tablespoon golden syrup
115g ginger biscuits
100g your choice of nuts, raisins,
   and dried fruit (roughly chop
   any large pieces)

1 Break the biscuits into small chunks and put in a bowl.

2 Slowly and gently melt the chocolate, butter, and golden syrup in a pan. Use a low heat and keep stirring so that it doesn't start to bubble.

3 Pour the melted chocolate mixture onto the biscuits, add the dried fruit, and stir.

Fridgecake can be a bit gooey so wrap it up in a square of cellophane.

4 Line a small tin with baking parchment and pour in the mixture. Decorate with extra nuts if you're feeling creative. Leave in the fridge to cool.

Some food companies are mean about what they pay. This means that the farmers and their families remain poor. However, the fairtrade label only appears on items for which the farmers have been paid a fair price.

Did you know that the first fairtrade food item for sale in the UK was a chocolate bar?

13 Winter crisps

These are much tastier and more exciting than normal potato crisps. The vegetables for these crisps will all be ready to pick and eat in winter. Makes approximately two servings.

1 parsnip
1 large carrot
1 cooked beetroot
1 sweet potato
2 tablespoons olive oil
salt and pepper

Root vegetables store well and are often cheap throughout the year.

1 Wash your vegetables thoroughly and scrub the skin so it's clean.

2 Slice the vegetables using the large slicer side of a cheese grater. If you don't have a cheese slicer on your cheese grater, make long curls with a vegetable peeler.

3 Spread your grated vegetable crisps on a large baking tray and pour in the oil. Shake the slices around so they get covered in oil. Season with salt and pepper.

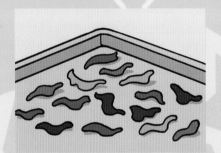

4 Bake in the oven for 2 hours at 130°C or until crispy. Leave to cool.

To make a great little tetrapod crisp packet:

Cut a rectangle of cellophane or greaseproof paper – 10cm wide and 20cm long. Fold the short ends to the centre and crease the sides.
Fold up the bottom edges and tape the seam and bottom. Fill with crisps. Then fold so that the side creases meet. Fold the top over and tape shut.

14 Energy bars

This snack will give you oodles of energy. Pack it for sports day or eat it in the morning before you walk, cycle, or run to school.

2 fairtrade bananas
125g butter
3 tablespoons golden syrup
75g sugar
350g porridge oats
120g dried fruit: glacé cherries, raisins, or dates

1 Melt the butter, syrup, and sugar together in a pan until golden and just bubbling. Take off the heat.

2 Mash the bananas with a fork.

3 Pour the oats into a large bowl and mix in the melted mixture, banana, and dried fruit.

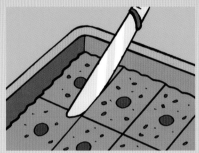

4 Pour the mixture into a greased tin. Use a fork or potato masher to squash the mixture down and push into the corners.

5 Bake in the oven at 160°C for 25 minutes or until a light golden colour. Cut into small portions.

Choose bananas with the fairtrade label. Also look out for fairtrade sugar, syrup, and raisins.

Wrap the energy bar in a square of cellophane. To prevent it getting squished, cut a little sleeve of cardboard (for example from an empty cereal box) and fasten with a piece of ribbon or raffia.

15 Popcorn

Many snacks come in wasteful packaging that can't be recycled. Make your own lunch snacks like this popcorn and save the planet one package at a time! Or make a big bowlful of popcorn and invite your friends over to watch a movie. Makes one generous portion.

20g corn kernels
1 tablespoon sunflower oil
2 tablespoons sugar
1 teaspoon cinnamon

Sweet or spicy? If you prefer spicy popcorn, swap the cinnamon for chilli powder, add ½ teaspoon of salt and pepper, and leave out the sugar.

16 Seasonal calendar

In different months of the year, different foods are ready to be picked and eaten. If you go to your local farmers' markets, you will be able to buy seasonal produce. This means your food won't have travelled very far, which saves a lot of energy. Saving energy is good for the planet because at the moment lots of fossil fuels like oil and gas are burned to make energy – but as these fuels are burned, they release nasty gases into the air that damage the planet. Local, seasonal produce is also a lot fresher and so tastes better.

Make your own calendar to show when different foods are in season.

Spring

Summer

Autumn

Winter

1 Put the oil, sugar, and cinnamon into a large microwavable bowl and mix together.

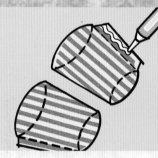

2 Add the corn kernels and mix again so that the oil is coating the kernels.

3 Cover the bowl with a microwavable plate and put in the microwave. Heat on full power for 2 minutes or until all the corn has popped – listen out for the pops!

Reusable popcorn pot:

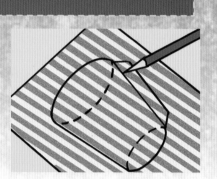

1 Use the template on the back of this book and cut out two shapes from an old cereal box.

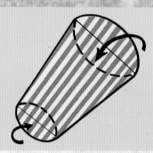

2 Glue the flaps together as shown.

3 Fold in the ends as shown to close the box. If you wrap your popcorn in a cone of greaseproof paper before sticking it in your popcorn pot, you can reuse it at least once.